She Confuses Lovers, Movies, Angels, and Poems

She Confuses Lovers, Movies, Angels, and Poems

Gia Civerolo

She Confuses Lovers, Movies, Angels, and Poems
©2023 Gia Civerolo
ISBN: 979-8-9893537-0-5 (paperback)
ISBN: 979-8-9893537-1-2 (ebook)

First Edition, 2023

Printed in the United States of America

Edited by Ghislaine LeFranc
Front Cover Photo by Gia Civerolo
Front Cover Concept by Riley Civerolo Douglas
Back Cover Photo by Jared Civerolo
Cover Design by Elizabeth Weinschreider and Emily Anne Evans
Layout Design by Kendra Foreman and Emily Anne Evans

For my mom, Jeanette Civerolo,
who read me my first poem.
All of my love, always,

Gia Terése

"You may have tangible wealth untold, caskets of jewels,
and coffers of gold. Richer than I, you can never be. I had
a mother who read to me."
                                                           – Strickland Gillilan

Contents

*PoMo Haikus: PoMo is short for "postmodern," in reference to the genre of literature that avoids absolute meaning in favor of playful, mini narratives that do not assume universality.

She Confuses Lovers, Movies, Angels, and Poems

catholic girl's howl
(this is not a confessional confessional poem)

At 13, she refused to go to confession
MAYBE
because by then, her sins seemed bigger than
the lies she had made up before

OR MAYBE
smoking cigarettes behind the grotto
in her black-and-gold cheerleading uniform
kissing all the boys one by one was way more fun

OR MAYBE
the confessional was a musty closet too dark
for her clothes or her soul with
a long-patterned shadow lacing her and the priest
together in a patriarchal, performative play

In that moment, she felt forever frozen in time
like statue soldier saints positioned throughout the church
always on guard, for what? She wasn't sure
reporting nothing they see while
their stone-gray faces always so sad
even with bright-colored flowers bursting at their toes
while warm, red candles flicker fervent adoration

OR MAYBE
because the scriptures
and Mass prayers were always
telling her she would never be worthy
or full of grace like the Virgin Mary
as the shards of stained-glass windows tableaus
seemed always to be looking down
stopping their stories mid-sentence just to judge her

But then, specks of dust fell softly like snowflakes
down the color light shafts
puddling on the marble floor
seemed like some kind of miracle

Even now, the image is a reoccurring visitation to her at 33
She realized the symbolism of her age
in that very moment as she declared to a stranger
pressuring her, that she didn't like being on her knees
whether in prayer or giving a blow job

Moments later, a laced, lattice-shaped
shadow lunged across the gray sidewalk
reminding her of the pattern in
the confessional a long time ago

She saw her 13-year-old self
in a plaid skirt
the hem not past her knees
always getting her another round of detention

A strong thought came rushing in:
MAYBE
that priest should have been the one
to confess all his sins
instead of standing in a blessed beam of light
atop a golden alter, righteously proclaiming
he was the only one who knew all of Jesus' thoughts

She remained strong in her conviction
to keep all her confessions on
the tip of her tongue
so you might savor the taste
without her having to say
"Bless me, Father, for I have sinned"

Now, she wears her sins proudly
like a tight, black dress clinging to her
without a shred of regret
And when the dawn comes
on angel's white-feathered wings
she rejoices, for she knows
it's the morning light that will save her
even if she is not on bended knees

jump-cut blues

It was always going to end badly
Fatal Femme Fatale lips
the red so luscious it leaks through
black-and-white 35mm flickering frames

Fluttering eyelashes with a purpose
shuttered through the light
of deep focus, wet night pavement
the kind that killers and Scorsese like

French waves jump cut
where even now
she still craves a smoke
to waft in a soft-focus haze
streaked black eyeliner
raining down her face

Some say (but not me)
a last manipulative plea
to the hero too weak for the title
or those deep-red-lip kisses
d
         r
               i
                     p
down white sheets   p
hanging out to dry   i
                                      n
by the Frolic Room   g
Strangling
Hollywood
&
Vine

flicker film

Death, the last flicker of film.

shock therapy

The feeling was jolting
like shock therapy

She felt you tingling
through her bones

Bones that for an eternity,
had lain silent

in a sculpted sarcophagus
succumbing now

to feelings forging to the forefront
caressing crescent moons giving

A sliver of silver light
into the darkened sky of her mind

Where you lay waiting with
whispering wisps of wheat-colored hair

Fluttering across your face
the image made her gasp for breath

As Eos shot the pink of dawn
she was surprised by the oceans of

Warm wetness at the mere
thought of you

words and waves

I can't shape words

I send secret messages in a bottle

Red lipstick embossed

Beaten by ocean waves

Foaming love letters

Out of Aphrodite's head

merry crescent falling moon
12/21/22

Crestfallen

Feeling like the moon
while the other
part of me is

Melancholy

Wrapped tightly by the night
shining and not shining

Chocolate-black donut
sprinkled with twinkling
Christmas lights
made of stars colliding with
colored planets
orbed ornaments

Reflecting against California white
night clouds and foamy ocean waves
substitutes for blankets of snow

"White Christmas" was written by Irving Berlin
in a hotel in La Quinta, California*
He was missing snow
like I am missing you

The merriment
I feel it in my shining half

Along with joy
even when "Joy to the World"
is not playing looped in my head
or strung along in a Target

It is in the breath between "Merry
Christmas" and "Happy Holidays"

Silent Nights

Crestfallen

moon

Melancholy

memories

Missing

you

*Then a Hollywood retreat on the original land of the Desert Cahuilla Indians

poems rage

The poems raged out

of me. A conflagration

of words. Fire rising.

TV in black-and-white

Your sadness flickers
like an old black-and-white movie
repeating on a never-ending loop
scraping the gray of your brain
an ending that still shocks you like
the final "Don't Stop Believing" finish to
The Sopranos that just cuts to black every time

Oh, why won't you please just tie it up
into a nice pink polka-dot bow
even though you don't always
like your endings "happy"

As a little girl, you were afraid of tornadoes
that never came
bringing black, twisting chaos to the still
swing sets hidden away in your mind

Did Dorothy really click her ruby red heels
only to go back to the black-
and-white flatness of Kansas
while you are aching
for the yellows and greens of Oz
over the rainbows that never came
with eyes desirous as the moon's

Switching channels on the TV
the reds, the greens, and the blues
laser lights falling softly on your face
487 channels later

you settle on *I Love Lucy*
because you do

Images you can live with tonight
despite them being black-and-white

petals and bones

I watch you sleep

through a female gaze

I struggle to remember the

names of your bones

I baptize each one

Grind them between

my teeth

You dream about

sea salt ocean waves

with pink rose petals

swirling around my

painted purple toes

I taste your allure twisting

on my neon tongue

Matching each breath to yours

still photograph

A moment

frozen

in black-and-white time

Her freckled face

smiled

the natural kind

She looked at the camera

My heart stood still

like the frame

may you remember...

May you remember the angels
with broken wings and rolled-up jeans
Kindness given without a thought to memory
Changing a moment (and your life)
with whispers of clouds wrapped in light.

May you remember the feeling
of bright days and blue overalls
swirling and spinning round and round
laughing dizzyingly.
Don't forget the look of love
on their heartache face as they pull
you in for a hug when you burst into tears.

May you remember the dreams that wake
you from your sleep with a leap of Faith
into morning mountain climbs
full of glitter star starts
sprinkling down in prayers made
for you on bended knees, or not,
Lifting you gently to rise
when you can't get out of bed,

May you remember
May you remember
May you remember

All the times I loved you

muses

The burst of muses

came whispering late one night

ink ran down her arm

i want my eggs sunny side up for thanksgiving
11/24/22

The house served heartache
first thing for breakfast

Yellow scrambled eggs
running from last night's hurt

Words pierced
through pronged, pointed forks
with slivers of silver
tender trigger points

That you installed
along with the lime-green
kitchen cabinets
Doors slamming!
Sizzling emotions
refrigerated ice cold

Toasted scars
burned blackened to a crisp
White powdered sugar thrown
like napalm bombs

Landed

We still don't
know all the
damage done
even decades later

While we
sit in smiling silence
eating breakfast

day at the beach

Walking by the ocean

Day changes

Clouds mirror waves

Sunsets take on colors

Painters wish they knew

Horizon stretches

Further than perception

Still, all I can do

Is think of you and me

Like there is nothing

In between

Martyr█

tonight █████ walking back ████████
███████████████████ I started
███████████████ chanting █
█ names of ████ men I ███ went to bed
with ███████████ burning ████████
████████████████████ chants
of names ██████ listed ██████████
█████████ didn't stop █████████
████████████ all night ████████
██ a spark ███████████████ not
████████████████ repented
███████████████████ father

Original text: "Martyrdom" by Andrew McMillan, Poetry, September 2017

van gogh's crows

The flying black crows

know which way to go in a

painting by Van Gogh

the bones of a black crow were caught in my throat

The cracks on the porch cried lined tears
when they butchered the shade of the elm tree
along with every screaming face in its bark

Spitting small pieces across the lawn that
no longer wanted to be green

Excavating the twisted roots
wrapped around iron and copper
secret underworlds where
only orange cats know

Squirrels tightrope walking on
the black telephone lines
condemning the chainsaw-wielding
weathered tan men
who were just glad to get paid

I could not look out the windowpane
The Lorax would be so disappointed in me
much worse than mad
I couldn't save a single tree, my tree

Nothing remained the same, grieving
wishing they had killed
the dilapidated house instead while
the bones of a black crow were caught in my throat

mother nature heals me
6/25/22

Lying on my back

sun camouflaged,

crying green leaves

through the trees

bright blonde beams

trickling, twinkling down on me

sparkling day stars

on a suffocatingly hot day

bashful breeze

refreshing me

like a lover's kiss

God does not need a name

to shine on me

not a hallmark card

I write epitaphs with razor edges, but
you still ignore me for all of eternity

I write elegies lamenting you, but you're still
alive asking me to move away from the TV

I write eulogies Jesus would rise again for, but you,
you always fall asleep at the best parts

I write dirges like pop tunes "with a good beat,"
but you won't dance with me

I write sympathy cards to myself hoping
someone will feel sorry for me

I write and I write and I write, but still,
my mind won't bury you

purple tulips

Purple tulips in

a vase, paint spring for winter's

buried memories

she missed going to the movies...

Curtain the color of
red velvet cake
opening like a lover
spreading their legs

She confesses to the audience
her guilt for how long it had been
a parade of forgiveness
cleansing her like applause

The lights dim,
lingering
anticipation of a first kiss
in a coming-of-age story

The white screen
stretches across her eyes
she projects a montage
of her dreams for all to see

She feels like the queen
in the scene
crowned again
in this consecrated grotto

The darkness falls
a quiet hush of a prayer
she bows her head
genuflecting to the altar of cinema

Escaping

Like any grief
she did not know how
much she missed it until it was gone
Now she is home again
the good heroine

Flickering images
flutter in her heart
kaleidoscope of
warm Kodak colors
melting time and space

Flushed frames in technicolor
containing moments
of mise en scene memories
never-ending narratives

The *fini* came abruptly
as it always does
bright reality lights
no more 35 mm
dreams tonight
Made her want to scream

She didn't want to leave
even though the usher
said please
pushing confetti of
popcorn down the aisle
showing her the
exit

She walked outside
the score in
her head went silent
superimposed into the night

She

was

determined

not

to fade

to black

climate change

1986

Last time it rained hard in LA.

A deluge. You. Me.

bff's.... not

Brightly braided bracelets
twisted tightly into four colors

Sharing golden glitter
broken heart necklaces
hanging in two halves that dip down
clicking like castanets against our clavicles

My throat throbs now from the cut
you made behind my back

Comfort and colored candy condolences
wrapped around the past, loves lost

Break ups, broken hearts soothed
Pajama party nights
Ice cream and champagne convictions

You purring
"I always knew they were that way
but at least we have each other"

Words not spared, like now
Whispering wounds wound tightly
around our pursed lips
Tears tearing smiles apart

Not a mention of our forever friendship
No longer foreshadowed into the future
Pitting a castrated circle
of friends called on to collect votes
choosing between sides or silence

i am...

I am stuck in thoughts scraping my brains

I am too loud sometimes when I listen

I am a wandering mannequin

I am sorry and I am not

I am a heart beating, rhyming with your tears

I am breath being held

I am a mother's prayer when you need it the most

I am a moon shining in the dark

I am a mother who can never let her kids win

I am stuck in the mud of the world's grief

I am sometimes who I want to be

I am an angel whispering winged prayers

I am a disciple of fate

I am the words between your teeth

I am a womb of creation

law-wrapped

Law-wrapped wire around

                her body. Betraying her.

She did know her mind.

my body is...

My body
My body is
My body is young
My body cartwheels across
the park's green grass
A WWI rusted, green cannon
is where I stand like a winners podium
waving at cars, hoping they notice me

My body
My body is
My body is swimming in pools
on my back to blue ribbons
My body still slices through
borrowed pools, 100 laps
Clouds stop to watch me

My body
My body is
My body is strong, flowing and diving
through ocean waves
Racing dolphins who stop to perform just for me
They fly through the water, away
no matter how much I plead

My body
My body is
My body is able to create life
Labor is worse than running a marathon
The prize smiles
Making your heart race, sing, and cry

My body
My body is
My body is getting old but still knows what to do
How to dance and move
Stretching across the past
Reaching on tippy-toe to the future

My body
My body is
My body is strong
My body is not wrong
My body is all I want it to be
despite what the magazine covers
might say to me

My body
My body is
My body is beautiful
My body is beautiful
My body is beautiful

my style

My style is chaos to calmness and back again

My style is purple streaks in my hair that fade away

My style is mothering with a wide-open heart

Wide open arms, wide open wounds

Wide open tears as you fly away

My style is flickering images with endings

that refuse to be tied up in a nice, neat bow

My style is love in a silent darkness that never fades away

My style is the daughter of a desert sun/son

raised in a Georgia O'Keefe painting

My style is a mermaid in the deepest turquoise

swimming with dolphins

My style is a rainbow of friendship that announces

itself on a gray LA day

My style is secrets that won't be revealed in whispers

My style is a child sitting in my lap while I read

the rhythms and rhymes of what life can be

My style is a cacophony of laughter,

one of my many love languages

My style is changing

My style is changing

My style is changing

even if you don't want me to

the angels were fans, too!
(ode to los angeles sports)

The California sun was dripping Laker gold
across the Dodger-blue ocean waves

Anticipating the black night
with a silver King's moon

TVs only tuned to victory
Charged city exploding
Screams of exhalation

Everyone could feel
the win reverberating

Ramming electricity across
the 405

Firecrackers

&

Shooting Lady Sparks

Clipper starships
existing only
on Hollywood Boulevard

&

in a Magic LA sky

ode to a band t-shirt, ironically unaccompanied by music

I am not sure what to say about my style
My wardrobe is all band t-shirts I've compiled
It is not shocking to say all these decades in
There are just too many stories—where to begin?

There are some rules:
Don't wear a shirt you bought just that night
It makes you look like a tool—no backstage invite
Reciting lyrics to their songs rocks the crowd adverse
Being seen as a bandwagoner is simply the worst

There is no doubt you must set an aficionado tone
You need to own at least three shirts by the Ramones
It is important to show you have expertise and attitude
Nelson (Ricky and Willie) The Stones, Tina Turner, and one with U2

Tell people you met Joey Ramone in head-to-toe leather black
They'll understand you were too starstruck to say anything back
He looked like a giraffe sipping tea from a white bone China cup
Later, on stage, impressed with your dress, he did hoist you up

Everyone needs one with Jim Morrison looking like Jesus
A statement many would find extremely egregious
Your Catholic mother no doubt gives a look of deplore
You can't help it—it's all a part of the rock folklore you adore

There are times you wear a shirt from a band you don't know
It only works if you pretend like you've been to a show
Especially if it's comfortable and has great silkscreened art
Mumble, sing the words, like they're deep in your heart

Not to be considered a poser, you must have punk rock creds
Don't tell, too many tie-dyed shirts worn while shrooming at the Dead

You must be sure to support local bands, then show great disdain
when people ask who they are and don't know the drummer's name

You can wear one if you were left behind and didn't get to go
Still mad at your husband even though it happened a long time ago
A gargoyle on your chest and gothic letters saying "Dead Can Dance"
He instead went with his old musician friend, "No Pants" Lance

Sometimes you might have a shirt you wear with pride
Even though, truthfully, you were only there for the ride
So excited you were but got too drunk to remember
Luckily your friend got you one as a gift in December

There are more stories with girls, guys, guitars, and booze
From rock-a-billy, pop, swing, classic country, to the blues
If I can impart one important lesson so clearly
Please love all your band T-shirts most dearly

eyes already knew

.

The eyes prophesied

the demise that came without

the attached warning

i remember ...

for robert 7/10/22

I remember the band screaming their loud songs
I remember they lit the Hollywood Bar
like a firefly igniting feelings of all possibilities
I remember the sheer, black-and-white polka-dot shirt I was wearing
with a black, laced bra and a white miniskirt
uniformed fishnet hose ending in combat boots
I remember you were wearing a 40s paisley tie
with a black shirt and black pants, your hair slicked back 50s style
with matching sideburns and blue, blue eyes
I remember sitting on top of a cigarette vending machine
with my legs crossed and a bird's-eye view
I remember you were quick with a light and a smile
I remember my black cat-eyes liner smeared
when I looked in the graffiti-filled bathroom's cracked mirror
I remember I had a crush on your friend who seemed like my type
Shockingly I was his type, too
(no one ever thinks they are someone else's type)
I remember the smoke-filled room made the bodies dancing
seem like Impressionist paintings
I remember shouting my story though no was listening but you
I remember you helping every band load their equipment
I remember knowing then you were cool and thinking
(not for the last time) "Just hurry up!"
I remember our friends who were there, and still are,
and feel sad for the ones who are gone
I remember you and I talked and talked and talked
I don't remember what we said
I remember thinking you were a "nice" guy
I don't remember knowing then that you would be my forever

love walks out the door

for greg romero the pope

I see you walking out the door
Eyes darting round for something more
Red lipstick and a tight black dress
Because of sins that I confessed

On my knees, begging you to see
There's so much love for you to flee
I'll put together your dear heart
These tears are real, tore us apart

Baby, please, come back, just remember
All of our kisses, oh-so tender
I am your angel with broken wings
I'll be your king with rolled-up jeans

I'm smoking packs of cigarettes
Smoke intertwining with my regrets
The clock is ticking half-past two
Fighting the thought that I've lost you

I crushed your heart of velvet black
No more praying you'll come back
I push the tears down for a while
Put on my old, cracked-mirror smile

Baby, don't come back, just remember
All our kisses, oh so-tender
I am your angel with broken wings
I'm still the king with rolled-up jeans

woman left the bar alone

A jukebox
plays

Flashing lights
cross sawdust floor

Vinyl
drops

Song
plays

Voices shout
LOUDER

Bar stools
sigh & empty

Mirrored woman
Stands

shape

Between the haikus,

there is your shape. A love poem.

Seventeen syllables.

fall forgot about spring

The flirting of spring
Blooming into surprise summer love
Considering it was meant
as a "meet cute" one-night stand

They got stronger, louder
Every day, 4th of July
Exploding love, BANG!
But it was in the quietness
where it felt most real

The summer clinging
to their tan bodies
Sparking kisses
glistening in the sun
Dripping down, merging
into hot blockbusters bursting
numbered summer days

The summer heat dissipates
into the crispness of fall bringing
an end to it all
She didn't remember surrendering
Leaves falling into
winter's snow globe blurring
all the promises made

Memory refrains
Popsicles, purple puddles
She can't seem to get clean
no matter how many times she scrubs
Ice cream truck's music jolts her heart
Parades of kids racing toward a future of
first spring kisses

summer + love

Summer lovin' underwater, sunburnt kisses
Rainbow bubbles floating by
bursting into firecracker
exclamation points in the sky
Names in sparklers spelling firefly letters
Surrounding by a luminous valentine
shaped heart disappearing immediately
Like a miracle, you can still see
hide-n-seek kisses, bottles spinning
Please land on me, 7 minutes in heaven

Summer lovin' dreams
Drive-in movie memories
Crackling, broken dialogue through
speakers screeching statically
Barely hanging on
We don't care
No time to stop kissing, not even for air
Doesn't matter that back seats aren't big enough
Exploring twisted bodies, double dates
Friends drunk in the trunk on beer, youth, and each other

Summer lovin' drips with Midwest humidity
for a split second too hot to catch
our breath or for any lovin'
Our bodies can't resist melting into sheets
and each other, needing a treasure
map to know where one of our bodies
begins and the other ends
as the cicadas serenade us

Summer lovin' sneaking out your window
to go skinny-dipping in the black of the night

as the mountains stand guard
Scattering starlight reflecting in
shimmering swimming pools
crashing into twinkling city lights
glimmering in the valley
Naked, we wave to the helicopter pilot
who just happens to fly by every night

Summer lovin' getting married
on the beach in Mexico at sunset
Barefoot dressed in white waves bringing
gifts of tomorrow's bright future
No matter how rough it gets or
way too many tequila shots
Arms wrapped around forever
Whispers of it will be always alright
I love you like a warm summer night

Summer lovin', had me a blast
Summer lovin', happened so fast

between degrees

We needed more than

73 degree days

Los Angeles gray

G I
A
█████████

The █████

The █████████
████ imagination ███████████
████████████████████
████████ giant █████████
███████████████
███████████████ being thirteen ███
briefly in love ████████████
████████████████████████ offering
██████████████████████
body ████ but not touching, ██████
██████ forgotten everything ████
█████████ remember everything—
████ tender, █████ gentle—
███████████ being offered,
██████████ strip down, ██████████
███████████ grace, ████████████.

Original text: "The Swim" by Gigi Marks, Poetry, February 1998

poets prayed one day

The words were wrapped, a gift.
Rhythmically emerging from the streets
to preach at pulpits that had not yet risen.

Smoke rose in cloud-shaped days
Resurrecting dawn dreams
through tunnel minds
Sparking light to the other side.

Poets prance through the myths,
history, stories, art, and time,
Shining words like a crescent moon
walking the tightrope. Connecting.

Bridging what is to be believed or not?

Trapezing from planet to planet
skating on Jupitar's rings
flipping down on glitter cracked stars
reflecting mirrors and society's tears
wrapping around twisted hearts.

Proclaiming past the black night!

hollywood dreams deferred

The look on her face
asked before she spoke—
"Do you have any
dreams I can borrow?"
She proceeded to precisely
pick at the reasons, like a scab,
Why her load had gotten so heavy
No matter how hard she tried to balance it,
she couldn't seem to carry her dreams anymore.

She asked again, a little more politely—
"Please, do you have any dreams
I can borrow?
Just for today, or for a little while."
She held her tears in her eyes
I lost track of what she was saying,
entranced by how her tears never
fell down her face.
They puddled in her eyes where
I saw a reflection of a me that I wasn't so
sure I liked.

She asked again—
"Please, do you have any dream
I can borrow?"
Her voice was more desperate,
out of breath. She had
climbed the hierarchy of hope,
letting her down time and time again.
When she made it to the top,
they only asked her to dust the light fixtures.

I became fidgety and searched
through my pockets, knowing
there weren't any dreams there,
pulling out change in the
hopes that it would be enough.
She only batted them away
saying, "I don't want your money.
I made it clear, I want to borrow
a dream!"
I watched the coins as they rolled down
the sidewalk, neglecting to pick them up,
like extra dreams
to give away.

She angrily spit out the question again—
"Do you have any dreams I can borrow?"
Her blistering beliefs continued.
She had worn high-heeled, glittery, ghostly glass slippers
that shattered into thousands of shards
She darted and dodged but still managed to get cut
deep into her toughest skin into her soul
No one was there to sweep the pieces away

I looked to the sky in hopes the clouds would take
shape in an answer
or that a rainbow would
spontaneously appear like a miracle I could point to
as a dream, but it was a gray LA day.
I tried to cough up words, but I sounded
as though I was choking on smog.
"There are dreams all around here for the taking.
This is Hollywood, after all."

She laughed hysterically and said—
"I asked if you have any dreams I can borrow,
and the best you can do is produce platitudes and cliché?

You think you are full of happiness?
Watch how the taste becomes bitter,
like this moment. You're wasting my time, and your own."
She declared as she walked away from me,
her head held high like one black high-heeled
shoe tossed on the corner of Hollywood Blvd.
where graffiti stars are easy to stepped over,
names that stopped meaning
anything to anyone
now.

I stood still, stunned silently,
wondering where did it all go wrong?
Where did dreams go for her…
maybe even for me?

A stranger walked by and I asked him—
"Do you have any dreams I can borrow?"

pollock

I cannot seem to

rearrange the pain, it drips:

a Pollock painting

spring and her awakening memories
3/28/23

Her memory, awakening after being
dormant in the shadowy snow

Lavender lilacs belonging
to her neighbor's tree
draping over a pale-green
childhood wall, even paler
and greener between winter and spring
Decades later, still her favorite color,
favorite flower, favorite smell,
favorite sensory memory

Petunias, bright pinks, whites, yellows
against the red brick of her childhood
split-level home where her mother still lives
Generations of little hands rummaging for
Easter eggs, the same colors as the flowers growing
along with those bright, plastic eggs
with bunny-shaped chocolates inside

Sweet peas, her birth month's flower,
springing throughout the garden
Ultraviolet blues, fuchsias, bright pinks
deep red lines, veins in the center
Mini orchids, real-life versions of
close-up flower paintings
by Georgia O'Keefe

Irises standing tall, guarding spring
Deep colors with a splash
of yellow, white, purple, violet-red
breaking up the same color monotony
They remind her always of her
grandmother's dirt-colored hands,
happiest, busiest in the ground
Nails always pristinely clean
when it came time to cook dinner

Goddess Iris bridging over to
rainbow colors of tulips
Whirling windmills of spring possibilities
and fields and fields and fields
of yellow daffodils
California wildflowers carpeting hills next
to the black coastal highway
She is bursting colors of bright spring flowers

Whispers of a cold breeze
makes her sad for a moment
Memories awakening
Remembering exploding colors
bright spring flowers
Their only grave sin is
before the heat of the summer
they die much too young

degas demands

The requiem for summer
Played softly in her slumber

Feelings unsure in darkness
Searching the sheer starkness

Trying hard to remember
What was it about September?

Watching dancers from the balcony
Degas dreams caressing melancholy

Trying hard to remember
Trying hard to remember

What was it about September?

melting memories

I sit with your memories
like an Impressionist painter
trying to conjure a masterpiece
with flowing colors and no apologies

I listen to the silent, blue sky
No sound of your voice lingering
Is grief gifting me a choice?
Petal emotions, swirling, scattering

I hung a tattered black-and-white photo of you
watching me try through my day
Everywhere, cracks of you slip through
Memories slowly becoming more profound

complicity

Another moment

of silence is a prayer

for complicity

Messenger

She took ▮ words ▮▮
▮ the words ▮▮
▮▮ told ▮▮
▮▮ loaded ▮ guns
▮ the words ▮ howled
▮ licked ▮ wounds
until they fell flat ▮▮
▮ bloody ▮
▮ death ▮
dressed ▮
to stop ▮
▮ desperate cries
▮ the poet ▮
▮ knowing ▮
▮ death ▮ shadow
▮ sobbing
▮ told ▮
▮ mourning"
"Who ▮
▮ you," ▮
and death ▮
▮ offer condolences

Original text: "The Messenger" by Mario Melendez (Translated from Spanish by Eloisa Amezcua), Poetry, *September 2017*

three words given
(battlefield, citizen, meadow)

The battlefield was

quiet. The citizens cheered.

The torn meadow cried.

words personified

Words are white feathers in a down pillow
I slashed with a knife, swirling them in the wind
Spreading far and wide
You are looking at me like a priest saying
"I've sinned"—telling me to pick up all my
words like feathers falling from the sky
Spreading like lies the damage is
already done. I cry.

Words hide from me as I stare
at the crisp white page
who day after day
would not come out to play
because they were scared
of all the things I might say

Words clung to me like a tight
black dress ignoring all your pickup lines
despite all your promises of a good time

Words come to me like the
sharp end of a dragon's tail
spewing out a conflagration
of fire
that could not be drenched with water
while the smell of gasoline
made them roar

Words sprinkled down like a quite snow
surrounding you with beauty, cold and quiet

Words were threaded together like a
blanket sewn by Grandma
giving me an ounce of comfort

while the grief and the tears
prevented me from speaking
I cling to it

Words dressed as Cupid
shooting red arrow hearts
so there is no mistaking my love
My love of words lifted
from the pages of books
tasted from the tip
of your breath
written out in a final
Hallelujah

mothers of many colors

Mothers bright blue like the sky
Answering so many "Whys?"
A smile turquoise as the water
with rhythm and rhymes
waves of words rocking you

Mothers serene green
the world weighing
heavy like a backpack
Voice like a field of green grass
on the other end of the phone
comforting at the first "Hello"
Words whispering, a cool breeze

Mothers pink, tickle pink
They know the secret spot
always making you laugh
Taking the pink hues of the dawn
turning into raspberry jelly
spreading it across bread
ending with pink confetti hearts
Lunch box love notes

Mothers red embers of a fire flickering
in the dark so you always know
which way is home
Red sparkling firecracker on a summer night
Lighting up, exploding encouragement
even when you mess up

Mothers deep purple courage draped
around you with such pride
reminding you who you are
voice breaking mirrors of fears

making it easier to stand tall and to rise
past the purple of the jacaranda trees

Mothers yellow sun shining bright
giving you light in your eyes
always in the shadows so you can shine
Cool yellow glass of lemonade droplets
of morning dew glistening from the night stars

Mothers a black blanket like the night
Twinkle Twinkle, you are a million stars
glittering bright as the world waits for you
Mothers the black as you close your eyes
sleeping, always there when the
nightmares won't let you go

Mothers brown the sound of the ground
giving a family tree you can climb
exploring where ancestors are rooted
flowing in your veins, giving strength
when you think you can't go on

Mothers orange blossoms
patient, imagination seeds
Giving food, water, light, shelter
All you need to be
Orange petals in spring mimicking
fireflies that dance with curiosity

Mothers white like a flash of
lightning that gets your lazy butt
out of bed and going even though
you grumble at the day
Mothers white light in a dark tunnel
whispering prayers all through the night

dead rose

Beauty true. Dead rose

in a vase with no water.

An altar to you.

just one more

The grip was clasping. Fist tight.
Just one more will take away
what's scraping at the gray of my brain.
I'll stop, I promise.
I'll do whatever you want me to.
Just one more. The last one.

You know I can stop anytime I want to.
Doesn't matter how many other times I've said it before.
I swear. I'm asking politely. Oh, so the truth comes out.
You just don't care. Just one more. Please! I promise.

What do you mean you don't believe me?
I am not in denial! You are!
I swear,
next time, I am not gonna say please or be so nice.
You're starting to make me really mad.
Are you listening? Just one more, damn it! Please!

I swear, rehab can't teach me nothing
I don't already know.
Honestly, I don't want to fight.
You say you want to believe me, then why don't you?
Just one more. I promise. It will be different this time.
Just give me what I need. Just to clear my head, so I can think.

I can look at myself in the
spiderwebs of the cracked mirror.
Bloody fists mean I feel.
What the hell about you?
Just one more. The last one,
I promise.
Please.

I will hum the lullaby you used to
sing to me. Will it pull at your heart strings?
I swear, I can make it all alright.
Just one more is all I really need tonight

Let me dive into the dark, deep silence of the bottle.
So, what if it's alcohol and pills? Who are you to judge me?
Living in your land of hypocrisy.
I will send a message not to worry once I've emptied
both the bottles and my soul. I swear. I'll leave.
Just one more, I am begging, please

You will never see me again. I can quit anytime I want to.
Fuck you for calling me a thief!
I thought you wanted me to take the money out of your wallet.
Just one more, I promise! Then screw you.
I don't need or want your money.
The last one I promise. This is the last time I will ask you for anything.
I swear.

As the merry-go-round goes round and round,
both too nauseous to stand,
you say it's always my fault. Everything is always my fault.
But I am still not going to say I'm sorry this time.
My laughter will blur into rage.
Just one more time. I swear.
Just one more if you know what's good for you!

My fist is going to go through this wall.
My knuckles will be as bloody as my heart. It's all your fault.
Just one more. I promise I will make it alright. I swear. Fuck you then!

Just one more, I swear. This time, it is different.
You don't love me enough to give me just one more.
I don't need you or anyone to save me,
cause I can quit after just one more. I swear.
Just one more. I swear. Just one more. I swear. I promise.

scream

She would scream if she

had to go one more day with

everything the same

my heart sings when I do these things

I write to listen to siren muses
finding out who I am along the way with
too many stories to be told

I read to transport into worlds I have never known
learn things I could not have believed
fall asleep with words swirling in my head

I take photographs to freeze a moment in time
stop memory in its tracks
Magic!
Silver and light see somebody else's soul

I hike in nature reminding myself of the divine
the miracle of a petal, world stresses release
with a breath as waves crash into me

I travel to see places and people I do not know
expanding my world with art, culture, and food
rearranging me from who I was before

I dance to punk rock music, swing to rock-a-billy,
sway with the Dead, go-go with surf-swinging arms
move my body so it remembers to be free

I do all these things and so much more
my heart needs to sing and express itself
wake up to love the day

ants crawled across notes and names

She forgot what she wanted to say

There was too much and nothing at all

The dead leaves began to fall

from the red roses in a white vase

Remembering the sad song

that played over and

over again in her head

She was all alone

lying next to you in bed as

ants crawled across notes and names

journals burn

Lifetime of journals burns really fast.

another morning mourning

Another morning mourning
Dead birds singing sweetly
not shaming how she feels
not shaming her into being okay
She always wore black before
She wishes she could paint
a red sash slashing across her body
hoping it would be read with compassion

The weight of the night is heavy
like a blanket not giving comfort
Your star eyes fade
She lives for the moment when she wakes
Not remembering you are gone
Oh, what a luxury just to feel the new daylight

She holds her breath hoping it was all a bad dream
Another morning of mourning
disappearing from the harsh light
She can't physically breathe; it all comes rushing back
convincing her, again, she will never get out of bed
She doesn't know what day or date it is
must focus on the month or year
Unlike a prisoner, there are no marks on the wall
just school pictures hung that will never grow
Images of how you would look and be
carved into her heart along with your last breath

Forced to face the day
the real world is a greeting of downcast eyes
High-pitched voices that don't want to know
how she really feels
Knowing they can get on with their

days, months, years, and lives without
having a hole that is never whole
for eternity
It gets on her nerves

She curses herself for getting out of bed
Those who share kind words and compassion
Who want to pin a medal on her chest for "being so brave!"
At the same time, exhaling relief that she does
not publicly cradle her grief in the shape of you,
the child she lost, like she could collect you from
the lost and found if she only really wanted to
She is beyond the reluctant heroine
thrust onto the stage
Nothing brave about mourning each and every day

Lamenting at lunch
sitting and eating in the park
she can close her eyes and hear your laughter
mixing with the kids on the jungle gym
The birds sing sweetly
Peace
She can breathe
The same breath ends and she freezes
Fear
rising in her thoughts
that someday she might
not be able to remember your laughter
it's just too much to bear
She collects her stuff quickly, leaving

Back at the office, it is easy to
compartmentalize as she always
did before
Just working
Not thinking
But that space never lasts

It's not her fault they don't know what to say
She still makes them feel uncomfortable
a walking tragedy they fear the most
She is a breathing reminder for them
She likes the days when they are too busy for
thoughts of her

Morning and lunch meetings
do not allow for mourning past three days
It doesn't matter much anyway
There are only so many things they can say
The connection with other grieving winged
souls are the only ones who truly know

Evening for elegies
Dinner and stories of funny things you said
make the family feel somewhat whole again
Pictures you painted brighten every wall
She can feel you there, smell the crayons
that lingered in your hair, the school scent
Now she is the one who doesn't want to go to sleep
She wants one more story, some water, to play with
the cat, anything not to miss the kisses goodnight
and the prayers to keep you safe

Another morning mourning
Seems there is only you in her heart and head
despite so much to do
All through the day
and the nighttime too, she knows the doll
you loved the most is in the corner of the closet
She can't bear to look at, touch it, smell it
It gives her a tiny bit of comfort knowing it is there
It will remain there for decades

Another morning of mourning
There will never be a morning without mourning

pocket gold
for my dad/civie
10/20/22

The gold watch ticks

Carried in pants pocket

Working across train tracks

Father's only gift given

graveyard

The ghost showed up in

the graveyard. She needed past

comforts of cliché

she went north on highway 1

There was no place left to go
The gods and goddesses knew it was true
She got in her car with the radio blaring
She didn't care which song was on
Fiercely flying up the Pacific Coast Highway

The Ferris wheel at the end of the line
Santa Monica Pier
Pacific Ocean waves
swelling and crashing
She remembers sitting in the top cart
swinging her legs, holding your hand
believing in all those Hollywood dreams
How we were gonna be big one day
right next to that Pacific Coast Highway

It was just past Malibu
she could finally breathe
She felt the lonely California breeze
The Beatles always know what song to play
Engine picks up speed
Coastal cruisin'
Tires shredding the blacktop on Highway 1

She ate the best hamburger right outside San Luis Obispo
The wind and Hearst Castle dominated the scene
She swore she could hear the mistress
of the house from those Hollywood heydays
laughing with a happy, "Have fun get going,
the highway is calling you"

Filming a car commercial, actors paid to smile
The traffic stopped dead, the viewing vista
comes slowly, the Blues were playing,

melancholy guitar notes
Cars honk to get back to their TVs
Content to watch the commercial
on their couch exclaiming their "awe"
instead of gazing out their window
to see the sea right next to the Pacific Coast Highway

The jagged rocks hugged the road
like a black biker jacket with an edge
She made the sign of the cross at the very spot
where your best friend was in a car,
when the driver forgot to cling to the curve
they dove deep to a watery grave
It tears her heart up as she passes by
thoughts roaming and wondering why
sacrifices had to be made for the haunting
beauty shaping this black highway

She settled into Big Sur like Dorothy coming home
The beat of her heart rhymed like the Beat Poets
They knew how to bend words like the curve
She climbed down to the rock formation
jutting, balancing above the waves
Took her clothes off, folding them neatly
Diving in the water, baptized again
She spoke a prayer to Mother Earth
When I die, and please not today,
fling my ashes along the way
Leave a cross as marker, sprinkled with bright
wildflowers blowing with the last lonely
California breeze on Pacific Coast Highway

where were you when the rain stopped falling?

Lightning slashed the sky
Flashing the Hollywood sign
for a split second   .

There was no thunder after
Another bolt cracked silently

Scarier when you walked away

She continued jumping
over, around splashing

in picture perfect puddles sculpted
by Beverly Hills plastic surgeons

Streams reflecting flashing
red traffic lights inside

spontaneous night rainbows
and store window mannequins

playing hide and seek
with her scars to see

if she still remembered why
by the time the rain

Stopped

F   A   L   L   I   N   G

grief and gratitude

I am trying to balance grief and gratitude
No one gets to play hide and seek
without the other joining in,
It is not a game just life

You were the glue in the family
The prophecies were true
Our hearts are broken
Dying in our arms
with your palm on our hearts

Days after your last breath
We laugh and we cry
You aren't here to heal together
the pieces

I am struggling to balance grief and gratitude
Packed suitcases stuck in airports
not knowing where to go
standing still watching the
carousels go round and round

I clutch a red balloon tight
before I let go
giving over to the attics in the wind
relieved that everything is gone
but memories of you

I am holding on to grief and gratitude
by my fingertips
Rising high and amazed
with blessings and dreams
I could never, ever see before

Feeling you there
watching me
the lonely breeze
calls me

putting one foot in front of the other
An orange rose
with red highlights
escaping a wire fence
giving me hope

fog

The green remembered

the morning fog, conjuring

its reappearance

sick neighbors

If you have cancer...
there are caravans of care
casseroles galore
chains of clasping hands
holding yours throughout all that
you must endure

If you have a mental illness...
there are eyes cast down
avoidance to be around
Good God,
you might be contagious
Your family is shunned
They must be the cause
Freud would blame it on the mother

If you have cancer...
there are calls asking
"What did the doctors say?"
research into medical treatments
meet my friend who is in remission
Offers of, "How can I help in any or all ways?"
The circle of family and friends
is wide with love and light

If you have a mental illness...
there is no discussion of what you might need
"How are you?" too scary a question
Being disconnected and isolated
while life scrapes at your brain
is where many people feel you should remain
Most of the time, even the doctors
don't know what to say

It's best to leave it in the shadows
where you should also lurk
while the stigmata of shame
drips down with a permanent stain

If you have cancer....
friends and family sit with
you through chemo, sharing
snacks and magazines
Mint-chocolate ice cream
brought to you day or night
Shaving heads bald in solidarity
The Big C is not as scary
with a cavalcade of support

If you have a mental illness...
it doesn't matter how many
times your mother tells you
"You are not your disease"
Police will still show up with
blaring red lights so all
the neighbors can see and hear
Word on the street is that you
were off your medication
which is true
You felt better

It seems to me
if Jesus were here preaching today
He would have something very different to say

breathe

Breathe, she said. Was I

holding tight? Frozen moments

I cannot get back

the light at the end of the tunnel
3/8/22

New, shiny, black, birthday cowboy boots

New Mexico night
Cities twinkling in the sky
Slashing desert red rocks
Lone she-wolf moon
Pulsing with youthful mistakes

New, shiny, black, birthday cowboy boots

On a slick silver track
screeching brakes
howl louder than coyotes
who know what it means

Stars glittering
thankfully
was the last
image you saw before
the light at the end of the tunnel

Generations later, she still
yearns in anticipation
for the whistle of the train
Haunting ghosts
holy or not
feeling lonely
coming round the wrong
side of the tracks
while wearing

New, shiny, black, birthday cowboy boots

rhythm of school

September brought crisp colors from the air

She missed the smell of crayons boxed with colors

Eraser clap sends fairy dust afloat

Scraped knees from recess playing, scars still here

Behold the books stacked just like colored bones

The teachers open minds to the unknown

If only time, like thoughts, could take her back

rocking in silence

for holden
7/5/22

I rock with your silence
The depth of it
The peace of it
The denial of it
The breadth of it

I dive into your silence
A tightrope umbilical cord
The mother-son connection
Trying not to let it to twist
Into disfunction

Worlds spinning chaotically
I yearn for your silence
A place only I understand
A place we can share
Where there are no words
Just our breath to quiet
the melting of both our minds

I lie next to your silence
Holding it tight
Trying to calm your body
Begging for sleep
Please

If I could, I would wish
First, for sleep to cover us both in silence
Second, I would dream that everything is alright
Just so people would stop asking me
What's wrong with you?

But silence lays stagnate
When words must be spoken
Silence a world all our own is a place
I must birth you from once again

How many mothers have failed
Desperately trying to save their sons?
Like the Virgin Mary or my own mother
I push the thoughts away, they fade
Words already unspoken
My emotions like dresses
I might try on again someday
In the hope they still fit

How many mothers cry silently in bed?
I won't today, I don't have time for tears
Sisyphus deeds are only mounting
Dread is stamped down with my smile
The unspoken scrapes my brain

So I am the one who must lift you
To this side without

Your spirit being crushed
Or being silently forgotten
I am the one who
Must pull the blanket of
Silence away from our heads

I am the one who prays in

SILENCE

movie

She imagined what

was outside the film frame. Worlds

beyond the red curtain

a movie, music, pain, and poetry
for Riley, 1/28/22

part 1

Was she just a character?
Your Mother's middle name?
Was she a feminist in past times that still feel like the present?
Was she responding to the constraints of her century's clothes?
Or was she simply a spoiled child who wanted everything her way?

The music would not stop playing in her head
Parading her like a whore then selling her like property
Across the world to marry a man who could not love her soul

Before it all began, they hardly noticed her silence
It was only when they took her beloved piano away
She had long ago stopped speaking
Now they look and pretend they want to listen

He played her body like an instrument
the pedal hitting the string marked by her silent screams
It's her body to do as she please
Do not blanket her in your shame
wrapped in apron strings and barbed-wire dreams

She pushed the piano off the boat, jumping in after
Surprised she saved herself
For her own soul wanted to play the
sounds of the bottom of the sea and sing

part 2

Those same musical notes helped me sleep
and give birth to my baby,
who will have her father's musical ear

The music and the movie play in my head and out loud
while the piano lullabies you in the womb
Your grandmother locked in a hospital room by the sea
watching the rhythm of your heartbeat
Novenas of silent nights and prayers

Three days of you trying to be born!
A clear sign you will not like change
(which you still don't, to this day)

You are in this world now!

The whole ordeal will change your father's goatee
from dark brown to ghost white
You will mark him as your territory
as you wrap him around your little finger

I am mouthing loudly, "More drugs, please!"

You cry!
I call your name!
You hear my voice!

S   I   L   E   N   C   E

Seeing each other's faces for the first time

This can't be right
we have been together for an eternity
a refrain that will always remain the same

The piano music calms us

then the chord strikes

L   O   U   D

Masking the cut of your umbilical cord
String stinging sounds reverberate
feelings transcend, underscored by the piano
Colliding crescendos of love around my heart
You are placed on my breast
We fall into the rhythm of each other's

B   R   E   A   T   H

The piano plays on...

a keepsake

The world came crashing down

She caught it with a flick of her wrist

Locked it in a hanging heart-shaped pendant

Bouncing off the bones of her breath

mother

I am a mother

whose love light burns, through my heart

while you fly away

she confuses lovers, movies, angels, and poems
4/28/23

Poems are like lovers
who surprise you anytime
be it a caressing crescent moon or
sun striking light on snow
slashing the day

Bright barbed-wire fences
where you dance
over, under, in between
perhaps a precision tango

Promenading away
pricked by a knotted, silver, sharp thorn
where a single drop of red blood
falls gently like a star-shaped teardrop

Expanding open arms of a lover waiting
an angel in the snow with tumbleweed wings
and words wrapped warmly like scarfs and scars

Barbed-wire rings on bare knuckles
where only poems and lovers can see and

K   I   S   S

so very delicately

the angel shivers at the thought
On a mountain top in the snow
where the highway is no longer black

Snow crunching
we try staying
in   and   out
of the tire-tread trenches
when it suits our past

Passing a graveyard
where a poem is being written
an angel waits with open arms
on a mountain top
in the snow
where the highway
is no longer black

and

your red lipstick

is a smeared kiss

giving a

much-needed

splash of   color

Acknowledgments

Thank you first and foremost to my husband, Robert Douglas, who proofread my poems in character voices like Captain Picard, Homer Simpson, etc. He always makes me laugh and gives me love, even when life can be challenging. Most importantly, he fixes dinners and the printer. My daughter Riley is a prolific writer and editor, which meant instant feedback and elevation on all my projects. To my son Holden, who keeps me humble. His smirk at my sports poem is the highest compliment I will ever receive. To my cats: especially Lumos, who we lost while I was writing this book, thanks for giving me love and attention and letting me know when a poem was just too boring to be included. I love my family with all my heart and soul.

To my extended family, including the angels above, especially my Dad/ Civie: you were the first to tell me your stories, many of which are hinted at in these pages. Your light, love, guidance, are around me always. Much gratitude to my nephew Jared Civerolo, who took the back cover photo.

To my friends: thank you for the many laughs, long hours of conversations, borrowed pools, fun, food, light, lessons, sleepovers, plays, healing words, music, poetry, dancing, movie dates, drinks, days at the beaches, books, camping and road trips, walks in nature, so much great art, and especially for the love through the heartache and achievements. You give me wings so I can rise.

To the many communities that have supported me and my family: thank you for your love, grace, purpose, and connections. A special shout out to the special needs communities, especially the fierce warrior moms.

I am most grateful and honored to thank the collective of CLI, beginning with Hiram and Charisse Sims for giving me roots and a roof with the Sims Library. Much love to CLI Session 10 Publishing Class, USC, for a life changing experience where all the poets were helpful, heartwarming, and hilarious. I am beyond grateful for the teaching and examples of Hiram Sims and our TA, Anastasia Fernald. A special thanks to my writing partner, Tasha Thomas for her detailed edits and encouragement. I would also like to bow my head to the past CLI poets. Their poems, performances, workshops, and friendships mean everything to me. I am beyond grateful to Emily Anne Evans who literally made this book possible throughout its production with her expertise, care, and understanding of my aesthetics.

The following workshops were invaluable to me with their inspiration and critical feedback for the poems in this book:

- The 44 Class with the inspiring teacher Karo Ska and the participants who became my first poet friends.
- Viva Poets and Merano Writers Workshop, who are writers with a capital W. Thanks to GT Foster for inviting me to these groups and always supporting me from our very first meeting.
- The Saturday Afternoon Poets, who are always an enthusiastic group. I'm grateful to Don Cambell for publishing many early versions of these poems in Four Feather Press collections.
- Be the Change and James Coats for an always poignant experience.
- Luis Antonio Pichardo and Abraham Jaramillo from Conchas y Café for their inventive lessons and the group of eclectic poets. Special thanks to Michelle Smith for introducing me to this and other open mics.
- The Anansi Writers Workshop and Open Mic at the World Stage where I am always so happy to be Wednesday nights. I am beyond grateful to the illuminous V Kale and the rest of the "family."

It is beyond a dream come true to call myself an author. Thank you, reader, for allowing me to shine as the writer I always wanted to be. I picture you holding and reading my book and it makes my heart sing!

Much Love, Light, & Many Blessings!

As Always,

Gia

About the Author

Gia Civerolo is a Los Angeles based poet, producer, educator, and special needs advocate. She has immersed herself into the poetry community for the past few years and is thrilled to have graduated from the CLI Poetry Publishing Class with this first full-length collection *She Confuses Lovers, Movies, Angels, and Poems*. She is honored to be published in Spectrum Online Editions, *Once Upon a Poem* Anthology, Four Feather Press Southern California Series Anthologies & E-books. She is also featured in the Bards of Southern California: Top 30 SoCal Poets. She can be seen performing at open mics most Wednesdays at the World Stage Anansi Poetry Writers Workshop, weekends with the Saturday Afternoon Poetry, and once a month at Pages on Stages at the Sims Library of Poetry. Gia is most proud to be Riley and Holden's mother.

www.ingramcontent.com/pod-product-compliance
Lightning Source LLC
Chambersburg PA
CBHW020420130626
46549CB00006B/2663